Lincolnshire's Lost Railways
by Neil Burgess

Text © Neil Burgess, 2007.
First published in the United Kingdom, 2007,
reprinted 2009
by Stenlake Publishing Ltd.
Telephone: 01290 551122
www.stenlake.co.uk

ISBN 9781840334074

The publishers regret that they cannot supply
copies of any pictures featured in this book.

**A Sunday express from York to Liverpool Street Station,
London, at Digby Station.**

Acknowledgements

I am indebted to my friend and fellow historian Richard Morton for his help in reading the typescript of this book and suggesting a number of alterations and clarifications.

The publishers wish to thank the following for contributing photographs to this book: John Alsop for the front cover, pages 1, 2, 4, 8, 10 (both), 12 - 13, 16, 17, 18 (both), 19, 22, 24 (both), 25 - 30, 32, 36, 38 - 41, 43 - 47, and the inside back cover ; and Richard Casserley for pages 5 - 7, 9, 11, 15, 20, 23, 31, 34 and the back cover.

INTRODUCTION

Lincolnshire is one of the historic counties of England, with Lincoln itself one of the four seats of provincial government in Roman Britain, yet to many people it is an enigma; several years ago a survey revealed that a large proportion of people questioned could not even identify where it was on a map. Situated in the east of England, it lies between the much better known regions of East Anglia and the old East Riding of Yorkshire, but attracts considerably less interest than either. In terms of its railways too, Lincolnshire seems a backwater and it is difficult for many people to imagine that it ever played any great part in the history of railways in Britain.

During the nineteenth century, things looked rather different. In a world where coastal shipping was an important means of moving goods – far more effective than the pot-holed and neglected roads – Lincolnshire's ports, including Gainsborough and Boston, were important trading centres linked to their inland regions by navigable rivers, the Trent and the Witham. The drainage of the fens in south Lincolnshire during the early nineteenth century created a region of rich fertile soils, ideal for the intensive growing of crops to feed the developing cities produced by the industrial revolution. Fishing in the North Sea – or German Ocean as it was then known – made Grimsby a major port, while further down the coast, Skegness, famed for its bracing air, became one of the first centres of mass tourism in England. In Gainsborough, Grantham and Lincoln there grew up engineering works, often initially producing agricultural machinery, but latterly a wide range of machines for all purposes, for use at home and abroad and in peace and war; the first military tank was produced in Lincoln in 1916, drawing on expertise in producing machines capable of negotiating the soft, rich terrain of the county's farmland. In the twentieth century, iron and steel production developed in the north of the county, centred on Scunthorpe.

All this development both attracted, and resulted from, the development of railways in the county. They arrived in the late 1840s and the structure of the main network grew rapidly, most being in place by 1860. Lincolnshire was within the territory of two of the main companies in England prior to the Grouping of 1923, after which date they were both absorbed into the London & North Eastern Railway. A broad, but accurate, generalisation is that if one were to draw a line from Lincoln due eastwards to the coast, the area north of that line was the preserve of the Manchester, Sheffield &

Lincolnshire Railway, which became the Great Central in 1899; while south of the line the Great Northern Railway held sway. Other companies, notably the Midland, might make incursions into the county, but it was the Manchester, Sheffield & Lincolnshire and the Great Northern which shaped Lincolnshire's railway history. Both connected Lincolnshire's farms and factories to the wider world, carrying Grimsby's fish to the midlands and London, distributing the potatoes, wheat and sugar beet products, exporting steam engines from Lincoln and Gainsborough and steel from Scunthorpe. The Great Northern created not only the resort of Skegness but also its most enduring symbol, the 'Jolly Fisherman', first seen on a railway poster in 1908. Not to be outdone, the Manchester, Sheffield & Lincolnshire developed Cleethorpes as a rival to its southern neighbour, the two resorts becoming the prime holiday destinations on the Lincolnshire coast. When in due course the company became the Great Central Railway, it was responsible for the creation of the deep-water port of Immingham, which it built from 1906 to 1912 as a rival to Hull, just across the Humber.

Lincolnshire's railways also carried goods and passengers from farther afield, especially coal from Yorkshire to East Anglia; and along its western edge ran the East Coast Main Line, one of the great trunk routes in England, on which, in July 1938, a world record speed for steam traction of 126 mph was set by the London & North Eastern Railway's locomotive 'Mallard' – though sadly the spot where the record was attained was only just outside of Lincolnshire. At its height, the railway system in the county was so extensive that it was reckoned that no village was farther than 4 miles from a station. When war came in 1939, many of those country stations found a new role as transit points for the Royal Air Force, which built many air stations from which Bomber Command carried the war into the heart of Germany.

The period from the early 1950s saw the contraction of Lincolnshire's railway network. Railway closures are today inextricably linked to the name of Dr Richard Beeching, whose famous – or infamous – report, *The Reshaping of British Railways*, appeared in 1963. Yet it was the decade before the Beeching Report, when its author was still behind his desk at ICI, that saw the closure to passengers of so many of Lincolnshire's rural stations and the lines that served them. Particularly between 1953 and 1961, dozens of wayside stations and branch lines lost their passenger trains and were left to soldier on with goods traffic only, though some lines had succumbed in this way as early as 1930 in the wake of the Great Depression. Attempts were made to breathe new life into many rural lines, or at least reduce their costs, and Lincolnshire was one of the first parts of the British Railways network to make extensive use of diesel multiple-unit trains on those lines still open to passenger traffic. By the time the Beeching Report appeared, it was felt that more drastic action was needed and under its provisions the county lost not only its branch lines but also a good many parts of the main line network, particularly in the east and including some of the earliest lines to be built. Before 1970 it was possible to circumnavigate the county by train, travelling from Lincoln through Sleaford, Boston, Louth, Grimsby and Gainsborough before returning to Lincoln. Today, such a journey is impossible and many of the lines described in this book have not only disappeared from the national network but from the face of the earth, their courses being reintegrated into the farmland from whence they came. On the lines that remain, it is rarely possible to travel much beyond the county without changing trains; even Lincoln itself has links to London only by changing at Newark or Peterborough.

It is easy to be gloomy about such a decline and to lament the course of what is optimistically described as progress. Lincolnshire does still have a railway network and parts of it seem lively enough. But its past also needs to be remembered and hopefully this book will help readers to recall the days when it was possible to travel from stations with names like Stixwould and Dogdyke, Tumby Woodside and Little Steeping, Stickney and Skellingthorpe, Rippingale and Twenty, change trains at remote locations like Haxey Junction or Honington, or brave the waters of the Humber on the paddle steamer from New Holland Pier.

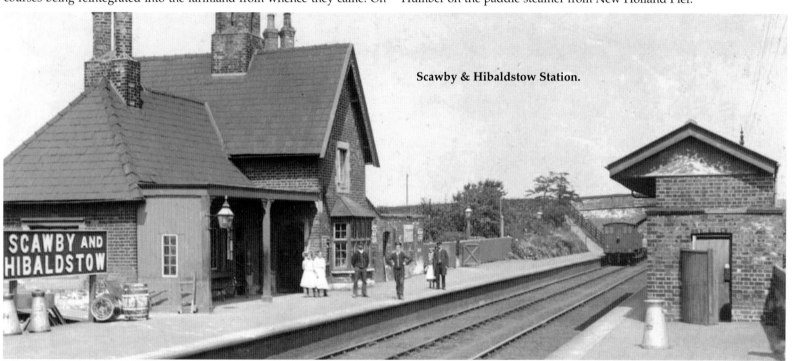

Scawby & Hibaldstow Station.

The Barton & Immingham Light Railway

Passenger services withdrawn	17 June 1963
Distance	6 miles
Company	Great Central Railway

Stations closed	*Date*
East Halton	17 June 1963
Admiralty Platform Halt	17 June 1963
Killingholme	17 June 1963

The development of Immingham by the Great Central Railway led to the development of ancillary industries around the port. The company built the railway in 1912 to serve developing sites north of Immingham, but apart from workmen's trains there was little passenger traffic and at an early stage a single steam railmotor was sufficient to carry those who wished to travel. Even so, closure to passengers came as late as 1963, while goods facilities were extended to serve oil refineries. The section to Admiralty Platform Halt still remains *in situ*, even though regular freight services ceased in 1983.

East Halton Halt, looking towards Immingham Dock, 28 April 1953.

Boston—Lincoln

Passenger service withdrawn	5 October 1970	*Stations closed*		*Date*
Distance	37 miles	Stixwould		5 October 1970
Company	Great Northern Railway	Southrey		5 October 1970
		Bardney		5 October 1970
Stations closed	*Date*	Five Mile House		15 September 1958
Langrick	17 June 1963	Washingborough		29 July 1940
Dogdyke	17 June 1963			
Tattershall	17 June 1963			
Woodhall Junction *	5 October 1970			

* Originally Kirkstead; renamed 10 July 1922.

Woodhall Junction Station, looking towards Lincoln, 29 April 1954.

Unlike many of the other large companies in Britain - which grew as a result of mergers of older constituent companies - the Great Northern Railway came into existence as a single entity, promoted in a parliamentary bill in 1845 for the construction of 327 route miles of line to link London with York. The bill contained provision for a 58-mile line from Peterborough through Boston and Lincoln to Bawtry, just south of Doncaster. This became known as the 'Fens Line', opened on 17 October 1848. From then until the completion of the direct route from Peterborough to Doncaster via Newark and Retford – the 'Towns Line' – on 14 October 1852, the 'Fens Line' saw all the Great Northern's traffic to the north of England and Scotland.

The line closely followed the navigable River Witham north from Boston and eventually killed off a good deal of the carrying trade on the waterway. Even after the 'Towns Line' opened, the 'Fens Line' saw a considerable traffic in goods, particularly coal, which was able to avoid congesting the more direct route although it did nothing for the road traffic of Lincoln, which was held up at three level crossings over main roads. Proximity to the Witham resulted in fishermen's excursions from south Yorkshire and Nottinghamshire to destinations along the line, traffic which continued until 1969.

Five Mile House Station, July 1953.

The line continued in use until 17 June 1963 when the section between Coningsby Junction and Boston was closed, Lincoln—Boston services being re-routed through Sleaford. A limited passenger service continued to operate from Lincoln to Coningsby, Tumby Woodside and thence to Skegness over the 'New Line' until 5 October 1970, when these were withdrawn, along with the remaining through services on the East Lincolnshire line. Goods traffic between Lincoln and Bardney was retained to serve the sugar beet works there, but goods services between Bardney and the Horncastle branch lasted only until 5 April 1971. The Lincoln—Bardney section, worked as a 'long siding' closed in January 1981 when the British Sugar Corporation ceased to use the railway for transportation.

Chesterfield—Lincoln *

Passenger services withdrawn	19 September 1955
Distance	37 miles
Company	Lancashire, Derbyshire & East Coast Railway

Stations closed	*Date*
Skellingthorpe	19 September 1955

* Closed stations on this line that were in Derbyshire were Chesterfield Market Place, Arkwright Town, Bolsover, Scarcliffe, and Langwith Junction. Closed stations that were in Nottinghamshire were Warsop, Edwinstowe, Ollerton, Boughton, Tuxford, Dukeries Junction, Fledborough, Clifton on Trent, and Doddington & Harby.

The Lancashire, Derbyshire & East Coast Railway was an ambitious project intending to connect Wigan with a new port to be built on the Lincolnshire coast near to Sutton-on-Sea. It would have run through Stockport and across the Peak District to Chesterfield, then on through Mansfield and Ollerton to Lincoln. The line would then have cut across Lincolnshire to the new port. In the event, only the 37 miles from Chesterfield to Lincoln were actually built, being officially opened on 8 March 1897. The independent Lancashire, Derbyshire & East Coast Railway was absorbed by the Great Central Railway in 1907 and the Great Central opened their new port at Immingham in 1912, effectively ending any possibility that the Lancashire, Derbyshire & East Coast line would be extended beyond Lincoln.

The main purpose of the line was to carry coal from the South Yorkshire, Nottinghamshire and Derbyshire coalfields into East Anglia (the Nottinghamshire field was still fairly new in the late nineteenth century). Although there were passenger services between 1897 and 1955, there were generally only four trains a day in each direction. The main use of the line was always for coal traffic and in the early 1960s there were still around forty coal trains a day passing through Skellingthorpe in each direction.

Skellingthorpe Station, looking towards Lincoln, 2 September 1955.

Skellingthorpe Station was the only one on the Lancashire, Derbyshire & East Coast Railway in Lincolnshire and one of only two along the line to have a level crossing over the road. It had two platforms, for passengers travelling in each direction, and a small goods yard. Like most country stations, much of its incoming goods would have consisted of house coal, animal feeds and agricultural fertilisers, while outgoings would have included farm produce and occasionally timber.

Goods traffic through Skellingthorpe continued until 1980, when, on 5 July, a coal train was derailed while passing through Clifton on Trent station. The damage to the track was sufficiently severe that the decision was taken to close the line east of the River Trent, rather that spending money on repairing it. The track was lifted the following year, though the signal box at Skellingthorpe remained for several years after this, being eventually demolished in 1985. The route from Lincoln to Harby is now maintained as a walking and cycle route.

Cranwell RAF Line

Passenger services withdrawn	1927 *
Distance	5 miles
Company	Royal Navy (Royal Air Force after 1918)

Stations closed	Date
Slea River	c. 1927 *
East Camp	c. 1927 *
Cranwell	c. 1927 *

* Precise date unknown.

Seen here with a leave train at Cranwell are (left to right): Tom Greensmith (fireman), Jack Mitchell (driver) and J. Fryer (guard).

THE LIBERTY BOAT

Cranwell Station.

Throughout the twentieth century, particularly during and after the two world wars, Lincolnshire has had strong links to the Royal Air Force – indeed during the Second World War there were so many Bomber Command stations that it became known as 'Bomber County'. Although their numbers have been dramatically reduced since 1945, and particularly after the end of the Cold War, there still remain a number of RAF establishments in Lincolnshire, of which the most prestigious must be Cranwell, the home of the service's officer cadet and aircrew training establishments. However, Cranwell was originally opened not by the Royal Flying Corps, as it then was, but by the Royal Naval Air Service for use as an airship station, HMS *Daedalus*. When the station was being built materials were brought in from the Great Northern line at Sleaford along a contractor's railway. When construction was finished, the RNAS had the line upgraded to carry supplies and personnel to the camp and the system was equipped with storage sidings, three halts and a shed for the several engines used on it. When the Royal Air Force was formed from the RFC in April 1918, HMS *Daedalus* passed to the new service, which continued to operate the railway until 1956.

Over the years the network at Cranwell was rationalised, the passenger halts closing during 1927. The line was mainly useful for goods, but passenger trains occasionally continued to run over the line in connection with special events at Cranwell, or, as in 1953, to carry personnel taking part in the coronation celebrations to London.

The East Lincolnshire Line: Spalding—Grimsby

Passenger services withdrawn	5 October 1970
Distance	47 miles
Company	Great Northern Railway

Stations closed	*Date*
Surfleet	11 September 1961
Algarkirk & Sutterton	11 September 1961
Kirton	11 September 1961
Sibsey *	11 September 1961
Old Leake *	17 September 1956
East Ville *	11 September 1961
Little Steeping *	11 September 1961
Firsby	5 October 1970
Burgh	5 October 1970
Willoughby **	5 October 1970

Stations closed	*Date*
Alford	5 October 1970
Aby	11 September 1961
Authorpe	11 September 1961
Legbourne Road	7 December 1953
Louth	5 October 1970
Ludborough	11 September 1961
North Thoresby	5 October 1970
Grainsby Halt	10 March 1952
Holton-le-Clay	4 July 1955
Waltham	11 September 1961

* The line between Boston and Firsby South Junction remains open for traffic to Skegness.

** An earlier station at Willoughby closed on 4 October 1866.

Firsby Station, looking towards Boston.

Legbourne Road Station.

On 1 March 1848 the 14 miles of the East Lincolnshire Line between Louth and Grimsby were the first part of the Great Northern Railway to open to traffic, the line connecting with the Manchester, Sheffield & Lincolnshire route from Grimsby to the Humber ferry at New Holland. On 3 September the same year, a further 18 miles from Louth to Firsby opened, followed a month later on 1 October by the section to Boston and on the 17th by the final section through Spalding to Werrington Junction, north of Peterborough.

The line allowed access from south Lincolnshire to Hull and the East Riding of Yorkshire without the need to travel inland through Doncaster, but it was instrumental in developing Grimsby as a fishing port, giving access for its catches to markets in the eastern counties and London. It also played a significant part in transporting the crops from the fertile south Lincolnshire fenland which had been drained during the early nineteenth century. With the opening of the branch from Firsby Junction to Skegness in 1871 and the Louth—Mablethorpe section six years later, the East Lincolnshire Line also helped promote the growth of the county's seaside resorts.

Burgh Station.

The relative decline in importance of places like Louth and Boston, coupled with the loss of much of the agricultural traffic to road haulage, made life increasingly difficult for the East Lincolnshire Line in the post-war years. After attempts at closure during the 1960s, including the Boston—Spalding section which lost its passenger services on 5 October 1970 and closed completely on 5 October 1970, the section from Louth to Firsby Junction closed on 5 October 1970. Only the Boston—Firsby South Junction section remains in use, as part of the line to Skegness.

Edenham—Little Bytham

Passenger services withdrawn	1873
Company	'Lord Willoughby's Railway'
Distance	4 miles

Stations closed	*Date*
Edenham	17 October 1871 (but see text)

This short line was not only among the earliest in Lincolnshire, but also closed long before the rest. It was essentially a private railway, like the RAF system at Cranwell, but it did briefly carry passengers so merits inclusion here. The line had no official name, but was popularly known as 'Lord Willoughby's Railway' as it was he who built it to connect his estate at Grimsthorpe Castle near Bourne to the Great Northern's 'Towns Line' at Little Bytham. In reality the line stopped short of the castle by a mile and actually terminated at Edenham.

In the days before local government, in rural areas landowners often took responsibility for constructing or maintaining roads and other local services. This was particularly the case where their estates employed many local people, either directly or indirectly, and the 'improving landowner' was a significant figure in many localities. It is a moot point whether this desire for improvement was a piece of philanthropy or self-interest, but it certainly produced some notable projects.

Lord Willoughby was clearly interested in contemporary technology and used steam engines in various applications on his estate. He also knew Daniel Gooch, who worked with the Isambard Kingdom Brunel on the construction of the Great Western Railway, first as Locomotive Superintendent, later becoming chairman of the company. Willoughby attempted to use a steam engine on a road he had built between Little Bytham and Edenham, but it was unsuccessful and he asked Gooch's advice on converting the road to a railway. This was done and the line started to carry goods from 1855. Because it was built over estate land it required no Act of Parliament, but when Willoughby proposed to carry passengers in 1856, he was required to have the line inspected by the Board of Trade. The inspection revealed a significant number of deficiencies and permission to carry passengers was withheld until the works were undertaken and the line inspected again. The works took a year and the board's inspector passed the line for passenger traffic in 1857.

For three years the little line carried a significant traffic in goods and passengers, but the opening of the line from Essendine to Bourne in 1860 took most of the traffic away. The passenger trains were briefly withdrawn in 1866, but were reinstated in February 1870 and continued until October 1871. Horses were substituted for steam engines for a year or so, but the line finally closed in 1873.

Essendine—Stamford East *

Passenger services withdrawn	15 June 1959
Distance	4 miles
Company	Stamford & Essendine Railway

Stations closed	*Date*
Stamford East	4 March 1957

* The closed station on this line that was in Rutland was Ryhall & Belmisthorpe.

Stamford's involvement with railway promotion is a cautionary tale not only for Lincolnshire, but for Britain as a whole. Before the Railway Age it had been an important coaching stop on the Great North Road, but was bypassed by the Great Northern's 'Towns Line' in 1852 due to opposition by the first Marquis of Exeter, who lived nearby at Burghley House. The railways killed off the coaching trade so Stamford declined while the cathedral city of Peterborough nearby became a major railway and industrial centre. As if to make amends, the second marquis promoted a branch line between the town and Essendine, on the 'Towns Line', which opened on 1 November 1856. The marquis was actively involved in the project and, although the Great Northern worked the line from the opening and leased it from 1893, there was a period between 1865 and 1872 when the company operated its own trains, hiring engines and coach stock from the London & North Western Railway.

The Midland Railway opened its line from Peterborough to Syston through Stamford in 1848, but they declined to allow Stamford & Essendine trains to use their station, so a terminus was constructed close by for branch trains. In 1950 the Midland station was renamed Stamford Town while the branch station became Stamford East. There was also a connection from the Stamford & Essendine station to Wansford on the Peterborough to Market Harborough line of the London & North Western, though this lost its services in 1929.

The Stamford & Essendine line continued to serve the town until the 1950s, but in March 1957 Stamford East Station closed and passenger services were routed over a connection into the Midland station until they ended altogether in June 1959. Goods services carried on for a further ten years until final closure on 27 November 1969. Stamford has, paradoxically, benefited from its nineteenth-century decline and is now a picturesque Georgian town of limestone buildings. Stamford East Station has also survived and has now been converted into apartments. The Midland station is not only still open but the building houses Robert Humm's bookshop, claimed to be the largest second-hand transport booksellers in the country.

Spilsby Station, c. 1870.

Firsby—Spilsby

Passenger services withdrawn	10 September 1939
Distance	4 miles
Company	Spilsby & Firsby Railway

Stations closed	*Date*
Halton Holgate	10 September 1939
Spilsby	10 September 1939

Spilsby is one of the many small market towns around Lincolnshire. Bypassed by the East Lincolnshire Line, an independent company was promoted in 1864 to connect it to the network at Firsby. The line opened on 1 May 1868 and was worked from the outset by the Great Northern, traffic mainly consisting of agricultural goods and produce. When Britain's agriculture went into severe decline in the 1870s enterprises dependent upon it suffered and the notionally independent Spilsby & Firsby company was only saved from receivership by being bought by the Great Northern.

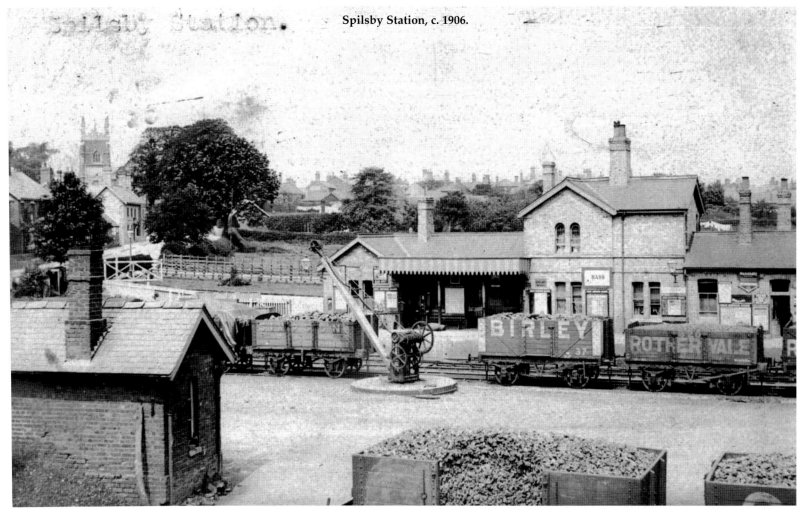

Spilsby Station.

Spilsby Station, c. 1906.

The line carried a modest traffic for seven decades. In 1938 there were still eight return journeys by passenger train along its length, but the following year, on 10 September 1939 – exactly a week after the outbreak of war, the passenger service was suspended 'for the duration'. Like similar suspensions elsewhere in the country, this proved permanent, though the goods traffic continued for almost twenty years after. The poor state of the bridge carrying the line over the Steeping River – immortalised in Tennyson's *The Brook* – led to the complete closure of the route on 30 November 1958.

Grantham—Lincoln

Passenger services withdrawn	1 November 1965	Stations closed	Date
Distance	18 miles	Leadenham	1 November 1965
Company	Great Northern Railway	Navenby	10 September 1962
		Harmston	10 September 1962
Stations closed	Date	Waddington	10 September 1962
Caythorpe	10 September 1962		

Leadenham Station.

Navenby Station.

Although the 'Fens Line' connected Lincoln to London by the Great Northern, it was a rather roundabout journey, having to travel via Boston. To provide a more direct route, a line was constructed southwards from Lincoln, following the base of the limestone escarpment known as the Lincoln Cliff. Opened on 15 April 1867, it met the Grantham to Sleaford line at Honington, where a triangular junction allowed through running to Sleaford. The Lincoln—Sleaford arm was removed after the direct Great Northern & Great Eastern Joint Line opened in 1882.

The line had five intermediate stations and at Caythorpe there was a special waiting room for the use of George Hussey Packe, then Chairman of the Great Northern, who could order any train to stop for his convenience. The route cut the travelling time between Lincoln and London by around three-quarters of an hour, some trains conveying through carriages while passengers on the others changed at Grantham. There was the usual local goods traffic in coal and agricultural products, but also, between the 1880s and the 1930s, iron ore was extracted from the Cliff and worked to the iron producing areas in Yorkshire and, latterly, Scunthorpe. For much longer the line was also used for trains of iron ore extracted from quarries around Colsterworth in south Lincolnshire and bound for the steel works at Scunthorpe. A much more prestigious traffic was the royal train, which was often stabled overnight at Leadenham during the 1940s and 50s if members of the royal family were attending engagements in Lincolnshire.

As well as regular traffic, the line made a useful diversionary route for traffic off the East Coast Main Line between Doncaster and Grantham. The stations all closed to passengers in 1962 except Leadenham, which remained open until the final closure of the route in 1965, after which time Lincoln to London services were routed along the former Midland line, joining the East Coast Main Line over a new connection at Newark.

Grimsby & Immingham Tramway

		Stations closed	Date
Passenger services withdrawn	3 July 1961	Marsh Road	3 July 1961
Distance	6 miles	No. 5 Passing Place	3 July 1961
Company	Great Central Railway	Great Coates Crossing	3 July 1961
		Pyewipe Road	3 July 1961
Stations closed	*Date*	Cleveland Bridge	3 July 1961
Immingham Dock	3 July 1961	Corporation Bridge	3 July 1961
Immingham Town	3 July 1961		
Kiln Lane	3 July 1961		

Corporation Bridge, 9 May 1946.

The Grimsby & Immingham Tramway was notable in two major respects. The first was because it was the only public electric railway in Lincolnshire, in distinction to electric street tramways which were to be found in many towns and cities from the early twentieth century. The second was because, unlike street tramways, it ran for most of its length on its own dedicated route and in this was similar to the 'Interurban' electric systems to be found in cities in the United States, which linked centres to outlying districts. Unlike 'Interurban' systems, the Grimsby & Immingham carried only passengers, whereas the US systems often carried freight too.

Immingham Dock.

PASSENGERS LEAVING

The tramway's passengers included considerable numbers of workers needed to provide labour at Immingham, the new deep-water dock constructed by the Great Central Railway – as the Manchester, Sheffield & Lincolnshire had become from 1899 – upstream from Grimsby. Immingham took six years to build and was opened by King George V and Queen Mary on 22 July 1912. While the dock was opened with great ceremony, and the Great Central's general manager, Sam Fay, was knighted by the King as part of the festivities, the Grimsby & Immingham Tramway had already been opened with much less formality on 15 May.

Horncastle Branch

Passenger services withdrawn	12 September 1954	*Stations closed*	*Date*
Distance	7 miles	Woodhall Spa	12 September 1954
Company	Horncastle & Kirkstead Junction Railway	Horncastle	12 September 1954

Woodhall Spa Station.

Locomotive No. 64260 at Horncastle Station with a service to Boston.

Woodhall Spa was one of several such watering places in Lincolnshire which were developed during the early part of the nineteenth century. Its relative isolation was reduced by the opening in 1848 of the 'Fens Line' through Kirkstead, a little over a mile away, and on 11 August 1855 the independent Horncastle & Kirkstead Junction Railway connected Woodhall Spa to the main line and also to the market town of Horncastle, famous for its annual horse fairs.

Traffic over the branch was appreciable, passengers primarily to Woodhall Spa and goods to Horncastle. The line even boasted a service to King's Cross in London during the 1890s, using a through coach transferred onto an express at Kirkstead, the name the station retained until it became Woodhall Junction in July 1922. Although operated by the Great Northern from the outset, the Horncastle & Kirkstead Junction Railway retained its legal independence until it was absorbed into the London & North Eastern Railway at the Grouping in 1923.

Between the wars the traffic remained significant and for many years the branch train consisted of an articulated two-coach set converted from two Great Northern steam railmotors (a similar set operated the Essendine—Stamford line). Even so, passenger services were lost from 13 September 1954, part of the great round of branch closures in Lincolnshire. Goods traffic continued until 5 April 1971, the trains being worked out from Lincoln and these were the last traffic to use the northern end of the 'Fens Line', which had closed as a through route the previous October.

Isle of Axholme Joint Line

Passenger services withdrawn	17 July 1933
Distance	31 miles
Company	Axholme Light Railway

Stations closed	Date
Reedness Junction	17 July 1933
Eastoft	17 July 1933
Luddington	17 July 1933
Fockerby	17 July 1933
Crowle	17 July 1933
Belton	17 July 1933
Epworth	17 July 1933
Haxey Town	17 July 1933
Haxey Junction	17 July 1933

By the 1890s the railway network in Britain was virtually complete, but there remained many places - particularly in farther-flung areas with sparse populations - which could, in the age before road transport, benefit from a railway. To meet their needs, the Light Railways Act of 1896 was passed, allowing for the construction of lines, either to standard or narrow gauges, which were more lightly engineered than would need to be the case for major routes. Signalling and station facilities were simplified, speeds kept low – a maximum of 25 mph was imposed – and instead of a costly Act of Parliament, the project could be authorised by a Light Railway Order.

The sparsely populated Isle of Axholme in north-west Lincolnshire was just the kind of area the 1896 Act was designed to help. The railway network was built by two companies, the Goole & Marshland and the Isle of Axholme Light Railways. Between them they constructed a through route from Marshland Junction on the North Eastern Railway line for Goole to Doncaster to Haxey Junction on the Great Northern & Great Eastern Joint line from Doncaster to Lincoln.

Belton Station, 10 June 1958.

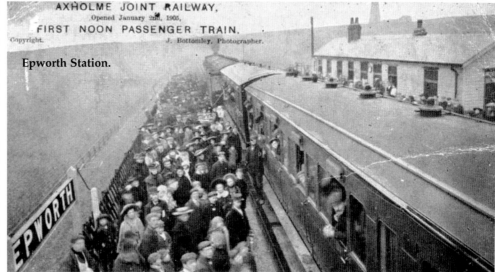

Epworth Station.

AXHOLME JOINT RAILWAY,
Opened January 2nd, 1905,
FIRST NOON PASSENGER TRAIN.
Copyright. J. Bottomley, Photographer.

Haxey was a strange sort of junction, there being no direct connection to the main line from the Axholme system, so it was more a place to exchange traffic than permit through running. A line branched off eastwards from Reedness to near the Trent at Fockerby, with the intention of an extension to Scunthorpe, which was never built. Another line struck off westwards from Epworth to Hatfield Moor, from where an extension to Doncaster was planned, but which also never materialised. The line's character as a light railway was revealed by the existence of an assortment of goods sidings along the route, some public, others private – seventeen in all. In contrast, there was a notable engineering feature on the line, the viaduct and swing bridge at Crowle crossing both the main line from Scunthorpe to Doncaster and the Stainforth & Keadby Canal.

The line opened in stages between 1900 and 1909, but from 1 October 1902 the two light railways had been jointly acquired by the Lancashire & Yorkshire and North Eastern Railways, both companies with no other lines in Lincolnshire. Daily operation was largely in the hands of the Lancashire & Yorkshire and from the outset the main revenue came from goods, principally agricultural requisites and produce. Peat, cut from Hatfield Moor, also contributed. The line passed into the joint ownership of the London Midland & Scottish and London & North Eastern Railways at the grouping in 1923 and attempts were made to economise on running costs, including the use of one of the new Sentinel-Cammell steam railcars. It was to no avail and the sparseness of the population and the general dearth of passengers led to the closure of all the passenger facilities in 1933, but the lines carried on with goods. In February 1956 the line closed between Epworth and Haxey Junction, the branch to Hatfield Moor in September 1963 and the rest of the system on 5 April 1965. The section from Marshland Junction to Belton was retained until 1972 to serve the Central Electricity Generating Board power station at Keadby.

Lincoln Avoiding Line: Pyewipe Junction—Greetwell Junction

Passenger services withdrawn — October 1983
Distance — 3 miles
Company — Great Northern & Great Eastern Joint Railway

There were no stations on the line.

Lincoln is sited on the convergence of transport routes by land and, since Roman times, navigable waterways. While this has all sorts of advantages, it can mean considerable congestion when traffic from all directions meets. This was certainly the case with railways and by the 1870s, when the main Lincolnshire network was constructed, there was too much traffic for the existing layout to handle comfortably. Passage of goods, and particularly coal, traffic - often transferred off the 'Towns Line' through Retford and Newark - added to the problem.

One solution was the building of the Lincoln Avoiding Line, between Pyewipe Junction on the line to Gainsborough and Greetwell Junction on the line to Sleaford; a connection from Greetwell Junction allowed direct running, at Washingborough Junction, to and from the 'Fens Line' to Boston. For most of its length the Avoiding Line strode through the southern edges of Lincoln on a succession of embankments and bridges and was long a landmark in the city; it also undoubtedly eased the congestion of road traffic in the city, abetted by the various level crossings over major roads. It mainly carried goods traffic, but also a considerable seasonal assortment of excursions to and from the Lincolnshire coast. Like St Mark's station, the line fell victim to rationalisation during the 1980s and closed in October 1983, the bridges and embankments being removed over the next decade. In many ways it was a foolish and short-sighted closure, since it could have been a useful diversion for freight traffic through the city, but little is now left to suggest it ever existed.

Louth—Bardney

Passenger services withdrawn — 5 November 1951
Distance — 17 miles
Company — Louth & Lincoln Railway

Stations closed	Closed
Hallington	5 November 1951
Withcall	5 November 1951
Donington-on-Bain	5 November 1951
South Willingham & Hainton	5 November 1951
East Barkwith	5 November 1951
Wragby	5 November 1951
Kingthorpe	5 November 1951

Donington-on-Bain Station.

Wragby Station, sometime in the 1930s.

In 1866 an independent company, the Louth & Lincoln Railway, obtained parliamentary powers to construct a line from the East Lincolnshire Line to the 'Fens Line' at Bardney. The project looked beyond the promoters' resources and permission was sought, unsuccessfully, to abandon construction. The line was opened in sections, the first - between Bardney and South Willingham - in November 1874 and the final portion - between Louth and Donington-on-Bain - in December 1876. The promoters had held out the prospect of mining iron ore along the route and even smelting it, but this came to nothing. The Louth & Lincoln Railway went bankrupt, passed to the Receiver and was eventually bought by the Great Northern in 1882.

Unusually for Lincolnshire lines, the Louth & Lincoln route contained two tunnels, either side of Donington-on-Bain: South Willingham (560 yards) and Withcall (971 yards). The tunnels caused many problems during their construction and the route was quite heavily graded. An operational oddity was that the junction at Bardney faced away from Lincoln, making through traffic impossible without a reversal. Passenger services were generally around four trains a day in each direction and came to an end on 5 November 1951, one of the first lines in the county to lose its passenger service entirely. Goods traffic carried on for a time, being withdrawn from the Louth—Donington section in September 1956, from Donington to Wragby in December 1958, and Wragby to Bardney on 1 February 1960.

The Mablethorpe Loop: Willoughby—Louth

Passenger services withdrawn	5 October 1970	*Stations closed*	*Date*
Distance	18 miles	Sutton-on-Sea	5 October 1970
Company	Louth & East Coast Railway/Sutton & Willoughby Railway	Mablethorpe	5 October 1970
		Theddlethorpe	5 December 1960
Stations closed	*Date*	Saltfleetby	5 December 1960
Mumby Road	5 October 1970	Grimoldby	5 December 1960

A 2-4-0 locomotive, No. 703, arriving at Mablethorpe Station.

Grimoldby Station.

Although Skegness holds pride of place among resorts on the Lincolnshire coast, Mablethorpe and Sutton-on-Sea have also enjoyed considerable support from day and longer-term visitors. However, it was agricultural traffic which prompted the opening of the Louth & East Coast Railway on 17 October 1877 connecting Louth to Mablethorpe, since holiday traffic had not yet begun to grow. Nine years later, on 4 October 1886, a second line was opened, connecting Sutton-on-Sea with the East Lincolnshire Line at Willoughby, and the two separate lines were joined by a section from Mablethorpe to Sutton-on-Sea from 14 September 1888. The Loop Line was notionally independent but was operated for the owning companies by the Great Northern, which finally absorbed the Sutton & Willoughby in 1902 and the Louth & East Coast six years later.

The Loop generated little passenger traffic of its own, but carried goods and, particularly at weekends, considerable excursion traffic. After the Second World War this was increasingly lost to road carriers and the growth of family car ownership and the line was closed between Mablethorpe and Louth in 1960. The truncated Willoughby—Mablethorpe section carried on until the axe fell on east Lincolnshire's railways in October 1970.

Midland & Great Northern Joint Line *

Passenger services withdrawn	2 March 1959	*Stations closed*	*Date*
Distance	25 miles (Bourne—Sutton Bridge only)	Fleet	2 March 1959
Company	see text	Gedney	2 March 1959
		Long Sutton	2 March 1959
		Sutton Bridge **	2 March 1959
Stations closed	*Date*		
Bourne	2 March 1959		
Twenty	2 March 1959		
Counter Drain	2 March 1959		
North Drove	15 September 1958		
Weston	2 March 1959		
Moulton	2 March 1959		
Whaplode	2 March 1959		
Holbeach	2 March 1959		

* From Sutton Bridge the line continued east through Norfolk to Yarmouth. A branch left the line at Sutton Bridge Junction and ran south, with a station at Tydd in Lincolnshire, to Wisbech before turning west to Wisbech Junction/ Westwood Junction near Peterbourgh. In Norfolk two branches left the line at Melton Constable, One to Norwich City station, the other to Cromer Beach.

 ** Original station closed January 1867 and became goods depot.

Bourne Station.

Although much of the history of Britain's railways has been made by large companies operating intensive services of passengers and goods over hundreds of miles and at considerable speeds, railway enthusiasts have always had a liking for the smaller, lesser used, and often more idiosyncratic companies whose services covered smaller distances and frequently passed through picturesque, but hardly very remunerative, countryside.

Twenty Station, 27 May 1937.

Sutton Bridge Station, c. 1909.

One such railway was the Midland & Great Northern Joint, which meandered its way from Little Bytham Junction and Peterbourgh to Cromer, Yarmouth and Norwich though latterly services began in Leicester. As with other such lines, its origins lay in a series of small companies, including the Norwich & Spalding, the Lynn & Sutton Bridge and the Spalding & Bourne Railway. The first section in Lincolnshire, between Spalding and Holbeach, opened in 1858 and this was followed by the section to Sutton Bridge in 1862 and then that from Kings Lynn to Sutton Bridge in 1864. In 1866 the sections from Spalding to Bourne and from Peterborough to Sutton Bridge, via Wisbech, opened, but almost thirty years elapsed before the Midland Railway built its connection between Bourne and Saxby in 1894, connecting the system to that of the Midland proper. On 1 July 1893 these miscellaneous railways, along with others in Norfolk, were consolidated into the Midland & Great Northern Joint Railway, ownership being vested in the two larger companies. They saw the Midland & Great Northern line as a valuable way of penetrating into East Anglia, the almost exclusive territory of the Great Eastern Railway. They therefore made all kinds of attempts to stimulate traffic along the route, including restaurant car expresses from Manchester, Nottingham and Derby, and from Birmingham to Lowestoft, Norwich and Cromer, while goods services conveyed the agricultural produce of the rich fenland through which the line ran. The line operated its own locomotives, finished in a striking ochre livery, and a fleet of carriages and wagons, all maintained at its works at Melton Constable in Norfolk.

The swing bridge at Sutton Bridge Station.

These attempts to create and sustain traffic continued up to the Great War, but thereafter the Midland & Great Northern began its long decline. Agricultural traffic and summer excursion services to Norfolk continued to produce enough revenue to keep things going, but the joint owners undertook various economies over the years, the most severe of which was the transfer of day-to-day management to the London & North Eastern Railway, as successor to the Great Northern, in 1936. The post-war boom in holiday travel was a windfall during the 1950s, but the need for extensive bridge renewals along the route sealed the line's fate and the whole system closed completely from 2 March 1959. At the time the closure of such a large section of railway, 110 miles from Peterborough to Yarmouth, was an unwelcome novelty, but with the Beeching Report, published four years later, it became the first of many. The main physical reminder of the Midland & Great Northern Joint line in Lincolnshire is the swing bridge across the River Nene at Sutton Bridge. Formerly built as a combined road and rail bridge, it now carries road traffic only on the A17.

New Holland Pier

Passenger services withdrawn	25 June 1981
Distance	1,500 feet (length of pier)
Company	Manchester, Sheffield & Lincolnshire Railway

Stations closed	*Date*
New Holland Pier	25 June 1981

Locomotive No. 61142, with the 9.58 a.m. service to Cleethorpes, at New Holland Pier, 27 April 1954.

In the early years of railways it was often considered entirely normal that passengers might not make the whole of their journey by train, but from time to time have to transfer to another form of transport in order to go where the railway did not. This was certainly so when large river estuaries were to be crossed, since bridges were often impossible to build and the journey along the banks to a crossing point could be extensive. The crossing of the Humber from north Lincolnshire into the East Riding of Yorkshire was such a case and in the days before railways the mail coaches had transferred their contents and passengers to cross between

The landing stage at new Holland Pier.

Barton-on-Humber, or latterly New Holland, to Hull. When the Manchester, Sheffield & Lincolnshire Railway was constructed during the 1840s, it included a section - opened on 1 March 1848 - reaching out from the shore to the end of New Holland Pier. Traffic from the East Lincolnshire Line could then be handed over by the Great Northern to the Manchester, Sheffield & Lincolnshire to travel to New Holland, and then across to Hull before continuing its northward journey through Yorkshire. During the twentieth century the ferry service was operated by a succession of paddle steamers owned by the Manchester, Sheffield & Lincolnshire, the Great Central, the London & North Eastern and latterly British Railways. The last of these, the *Wingfield Castle*, *Tattershall Castle* and *Lincoln Castle*, were built between 1934 and 1940, the latter steamer remaining in service until 1978. The final vessel used on the service was the MV *Farringford*, a former Southern Railway ferry built to serve the Isle of Wight from Lymington. The writing was on the wall for the ferries since construction work on the Humber road bridge had begun in 1973 and this was finally opened on 24 June 1981. The next day the railway along the pier closed and the structure was converted to carry pipelines. It still exists, as do the three 'Castles', all having been converted into floating restaurants.

The 'New Line': Coningsby Junction—Bellwater Junction

Passenger services withdrawn	5 October 1970	*Stations closed*	*Date*
Distance	15 miles	Tumby Woodside	5 October 1970
Company	Great Northern Railway	New Bolingbroke	5 October 1970
		Stickney	5 October 1970
		Midville	5 October 1970
Stations closed	*Date*		
Coningsby	5 October 1970		

Stickney Station.

The creation of Skegness and other Lincolnshire coast resorts as major tourist destinations during the latter part of the nineteenth century, and their popularity with people from south Yorkshire, Derbyshire and Nottinghamshire, emphasised the lack of a direct route between Lincoln and the coast via the 'Fens Line'. To remedy this a connection between the 'Fens Line' at Coningsby Junction and the East Lincolnshire Line at Bellwater Junction was opened on 1 July 1913, the last major route to be built in the county and thus the reason for its nickname, the 'New Line'. Double track throughout, it was primarily a through route and for much of its life the five stations along it were served by only four passenger trains a day in each direction. During the First World War, one line of track was removed to be sent to France for military railways serving the Western Front, but after the war double track was restored. Although it carried a good deal of seasonal traffic, it fell victim to rationalisation during the 1960s and was closed completely in 1970. Its demise meant that journeys from Lincoln to Skegness now went via Sleaford and Boston, a longer route than the one the 'New Line' had been built to reduce almost sixty years before.

Retford—Saxilby via Torksey *

Passenger services withdrawn	2 November 1959
Distance	8 miles
Company	Manchester, Sheffield & Lincolnshire Railway

Stations closed	Date
Torksey	2 November 1959

* Closed stations on this line that were in Nottinghamshire were Leverton and Cottam.

The Manchester, Sheffield & Lincolnshire Railway route from Sheffield ran into Lincolnshire via Gainsborough, making its way from there to Brigg and Grimsby on a line that was opened in July 1849. The company also wished to run from Sheffield to Lincoln and there make an end-on connection with its line from Barnetby via Market Rasen, which had opened in December 1848. Doing this required the co-operation of the Great Northern, which had recently arrived in the city and which opened its line northwards through Gainsborough to Doncaster, also in 1849. Having reached agreement with the Great Northern, the Manchester, Sheffield & Lincolnshire constructed an 8-mile line from Clarborough Junction in Nottinghamshire to Sykes Junction, just north of Saxilby, crossing the Trent at Torksey by means of an impressive plate-girder bridge.

Although the route was an important link between Sheffield and Lincoln, it was closed in November 1959 and its traffic diverted along the original Manchester, Sheffield & Lincolnshire line to Gainsborough and then down the Great Northern line to Lincoln. Track on the section across the Trent at Torksey was removed, but the line from Sykes Junction to Torksey remained in use until 1988 in order to serve an oil terminal on the river. The opening of a coal-fired power station on the west bank of the Trent at Cottam in 1968 meant that the section from Clarborough Junction to the power station was relaid for 'merry-go-round' trains from the Nottinghamshire and South Yorkshire pits. This last section, along with the unused Trent bridge, still remain.

Saxby – Bourne *

Passenger services withdrawn	2 March 1959
Distance	18 miles
Company	Midland Railway

Stations closed	Date
South Witham	2 March 1959
Castle Bytham	2 March 1959
Bourne	2 March 1959

* The closed station on this line that was in Leicestershire was Edmondthorpe & Wymondham.

The Midland Railway spent a good deal of time and effort over the years attempting to break out of its home territory in central England and particularly in trying to build or gain control of routes to the coast. This was sometimes done in collaboration with other companies in order to break into the territory of a third; one has only to think of its alliance with the London & South Western to gain control of the Somerset & Dorset line and so cut across the Great Western to reach Bournemouth. A similar alliance with the Great Northern made it a partner in the Midland & Great Northern Joint [qv] by which it gained access to Norfolk in the teeth of opposition from the Great Eastern.

In 1890 the Midland gained parliamentary powers to construct a line from Saxby Junction, on its route from Nottingham to Wellingborough, via Melton Mowbray and Oakham, to make an end-on connection with the Midland & Great Northern at Bourne. In fact, the latter company actually owned the section from east of Castle Bytham to Bourne, though the remainder of the route was Midland property. It was opened to goods traffic in 1893 and to passengers in the following year, and provided a route from Leicester to the Norfolk coast. Into the 1950s it had a service of four passenger trains a day in each direction, boosted on summer Saturdays with excursions and special workings. It was almost wholly bound up with the Midland & Great Northern Joint and suffered the same fate, along with it closing to passengers in March 1959. Goods traffic continued until 1964. Earthworks along some parts of the route can still be seen, not least a most impressive embankment and underbridge next to the East Coast Main Line at Little Bytham.

St Mark's Station

Passenger services withdrawn	12 May 1985
Distance	1 mile (approx.)
Company	Midland Railway

Stations closed	*Date*
Lincoln St Marks	13 May 1985

Although Lincolnshire was predominantly in the territory of the Manchester, Sheffield & Lincolnshire and the Great Northern Railways, the Midland was the first to operate a service in the county and to connect the city of Lincoln to the railway network. On 3 August 1846, the company formally opened its line from Nottingham via Newark to a terminus in the parish of St Mark, Lincoln, after which the station was known. Two years later it became a through station, the Manchester, Sheffield & Lincolnshire laying a connecting line to the station from Pelham Street junction, so permitting through running and transfer of traffic from Grimsby to Nottingham; it also added another level crossing to the High Street. Around St Mark's Station grew up a network of lines serving a wide range of industries in central Lincoln and this became the Midland's railhead in Lincolnshire. The company clearly thought well of their line as the city's coat of arms became one of six, along with Birmingham, Derby, Leeds, Bristol and Leicester, incorporated into the Midland's own arms.

St Mark's fell victim to rationalisation of the railway network in Lincoln during the 1980s. The station, along with the connection to the Grimsby line and almost a mile of line west of the station, was closed and trains from Nottingham re-routed into the Central station using a new connecting spur from Boultham Junction to West Holmes on the line to Gainsborough. The Midland trackbed disappeared under redevelopment of the old central industrial area but the main station building has been incorporated into a new shopping centre. Even St Mark's Church has gone, another victim of rationalisation – in this case by the Church of England – in the 1970s.

A 0-6-0 locomotive, No. 453, built in 1860 and seen here at St Mark's Station.

Scunthorpe—Whitton

Passenger services withdrawn	13 July 1925	*Stations closed*	*Date*
Distance	11 miles	Scunthorpe	13 July 1925
Company	North Lindsey Light Railway	Winterton & Thealby	13 July 1925
		West Halton	13 July 1925
		Winteringham	13 July 1925
		Whitton	13 July 1925

A 0-6-0 locomotive, No. 498, at Winterton & Thealby Station, c. 1905.

Lincolnshire is generally thought of as a rural county, dependent on agriculture, but throughout the nineteenth century there was a strong tradition of engineering, particularly in centres like Lincoln, Gainsborough and Grantham, and the latter part of the century saw the development of iron and steel making on the southern bank of the Humber. Iron ore was extracted in the area around Frodingham from 1860; iron making began four years later and steel production began in 1890. Ore could also be imported through the Humber, but the two world wars encouraged greater use of home resources, even though the ore yielded a relatively low iron content. By 1968, Scunthorpe accounted for 11.8% of the steel produced in Britain.

It was iron ore extraction in the area between Scunthorpe and the Humber which prompted the construction of a light railway, initially between Scunthorpe and West Halton, then to Winteringham Haven and finally, after a reversal, to Whitton on the Humber bank. The original scheme to construct the line was promoted by local iron masters, but construction was undertaken by the Great Central Railway, anxious to keep out the Lancashire & Yorkshire Railway, which had gained access to the area to the west of the Trent by its involvement in the Axholme Joint system. The North Lindsey Light Railway opened in September 1906 and was worked by the Great Central from the outset.

Unsurprisingly, the main traffic over the line was mineral goods, mainly coal and iron ore, and the passenger service was minimal, only three trains each way daily, later reduced to two. Passenger traffic ceased in May 1925, but goods carried on for much longer. Whitton and Winteringham lost their trains from 1 October 1951, with West Halton seeing its last working on 29 May 1961 and Winterton holding out until 20 July 1964. Even this was not the end as the southern section continued to be worked by the British Steel Corporation until August 1980 and the rails were still in situ until relatively recently.

Sleaford—Bourne

			Date
Passenger services withdrawn	22 September 1930	Stations closed	
Distance	16 miles	Aswarby for Scredington	22 September 1930
Company	Great Northern Railway	Billingborough & Horbling	22 September 1930
		Rippingale	22 September 1930
		Morton Road	22 September 1930

Billingborough Station.

Railways were promoted for a variety of reasons, but in most cases those promoting them believed that they would be of some commercial benefit. Occasionally, however, promoters realised before construction began that there was no realistic hope of a return on their money; but, just as a railway line needed to be authorised by Act of Parliament, an abandonment of construction also required parliamentary approval. The Great Northern line from Sleaford to Bourne was such a case. Authorised in 1865, three years later the company petitioned Parliament to be allowed not to proceed with the works; but just as Parliament could refuse permission to construct, they could also refuse permission to abandon and this they did. The single line was opened to goods in October 1871 and to passengers in January 1872, but traffic was sparse and connections for other services at the ends of the line were poor. Less than fifty years later, on 22 September 1930, the London & North Eastern Railway withdrew passenger services on the line, the final blow being struck by the need for economies in the wake of the Great Depression of the previous year. Even so, for nine more years excursions to Skegness called at the stations and these remained in good repair, despite closure. Indeed, at least one observer recalled that they received blue enamel name signs in British Railways days, despite there being no passengers to read them!

Although passenger services disappeared early, as with so many other branches goods lingered on. A daily train ran the length of the line until 28 July 1956, when the section from Sleaford to Billingborough closed completely. Even then all was not finished, because the line was used to store redundant wagons – a use to which other lines were put at the time. The truncated line from Bourne to Billingborough remained open for goods until 2 April 1965.

Spalding—March *

Passenger services withdrawn	11 September 1961
Distance	19 miles
Company	Great Northern Railway

Stations closed	Date
Cowbit	11 September 1961
Postland	11 September 1961
French Drove & Gedney Hill	11 September 1961

* Closed stations on this line that were in Cambridgeshire were Murrow and Guyhirne.

Just as the Great Northern Railway held sway over the southern half of Lincolnshire, so the Great Eastern Railway enjoyed an effective monopoly over the Wash in East Anglia, right down to the Essex bank of the Thames. The Great Eastern provided a varied selection of services, from tightly timed London suburban services to quiet branch lines in Norfolk and Suffolk, but it had no direct access to the lucrative traffic from the coalfields of the midlands and Yorkshire. The logical route northwards seemed to be from March in Cambridgeshire into Lincolnshire, making contact with the East Lincolnshire Line between Peterborough and Boston. The Great Northern, as anxious to defend its territory as the Great Eastern was to enter it, countered by building a line from Spalding to March, which opened in 1867. Thus the Great Eastern could receive traffic from the Great Northern at March, but this only whetted its appetite further and a direct line from Spalding to Lincoln was proposed in 1876.

The Great Northern, realising that the best way of tackling the matter was by agreement rather than confrontation and, no doubt depending on the reality that the Great Eastern could only reach a line of its own from Spalding by gaining running powers over the Great Northern line from March, negotiated a compromise. A Spalding to Lincoln line would be built jointly by the two companies, and the existing Great Northern lines between Doncaster and Lincoln, and Spalding and Peterborough – along with several connecting lines in Huntingdonshire – would become the Great Northern & Great Eastern Joint line. The Spalding to Lincoln section included the Lincoln avoiding line and the whole network consisted of 122 miles of railway, opening to traffic in 1882.

Although the Great Northern might be seen to have made no small concession to accommodate the Great Eastern, it benefited both from a share in the revenue of the coal traffic for East Anglia and also avoided the need to route this over its own lines south of Lincoln, or else allow it passage to Peterborough down the East Coast Main Line. The Joint Line was the making of March as a major railway centre and for a century the line carried a vast volume of traffic. The dependence on goods traffic was underlined by the early closure to passengers of the five intermediate stations between Spalding and March, though through trains continued over the route, but in 1982 British Railways decided that it wished to close this section entirely and route traffic for March through Peterborough. The closure was effected in November of that year, the changes in freight traffic having already been reflected by the closure of the Down yard at March ten years earlier. Although with many intermediate stations closed and local goods services withdrawn, the majority of the Joint line north of Spalding remains open to traffic.

Stations closed on lines still open to passengers

Barnetby—Doncaster

Company	Manchester, Sheffield & Lincolnshire Railway

Stations closed	*Date*
Appleby	5 June 1967

Doncaster—Peterborough

Company	Great Northern Railway

Stations closed	*Date*
Finningley	11 September 1961
Park Drain	7 February 1955
Haxey Junction	17 July 1933
Misterton	11 September 1961
Walkeringham	2 February 1959
Beckingham	2 November 1959
Lea	6 August 1957
Stow Park	11 September 1961
Branston & Heighington	3 November 1958
Potterhanworth	2 May 1955
Nocton & Dunston	2 May 1955

Stations closed	*Date*
Scopwick & Timberland	7 November 1955
Digby	11 September 1961
Helpringham	4 July 1955
Donington Road	11 September 1961
Gosberton	11 September 1961
Pinchbeck	11 September 1961
Littleworth *	11 September 1961
St James Deeping *	11 September 1961
Peakirk *	11 September 1961

* After other stations on the line were taken over by the Great Northern & Great Eastern Joint, these remained with the Great Northern Railway until Grouping in 1923.

Lea Station.

Pinchbeck Station, c. 1909.

PINCHBECK STATION

602

Donington Road Station.

DONINGTON STATION

561

East Coast Main Line: Newark—Peterborough

Company		Great Northern Railway	Stations closed	Date
			Corby Glen	15 June 1959
Stations closed		*Date*	Little Bytham	15 June 1959
Claypole		16 September 1957	Essendine *	15 June 1959
Hougham		16 September 1957	Tallington	15 June 1959
Barkston		16 March 1955		
Great Ponton		15 September 1958		

* The closed station on this line that was in Rutland was Essendine.

Tallington Station.

Firsby Junction—Skegness

Company   Great Northern Railway

Stations closed	*Date*
Seacroft	3 December 1953

Gainsborough—Barnetby

Company   Manchester, Sheffield & Lincolnshire Railway

Stations closed	*Date*
Blyton	2 February 1959
Northorpe	4 July 1955
Scawby & Hibaldstow	5 February 1968

Lincoln—Cleethorpes

Company   Manchester, Sheffield & Lincolnshire Railway

Stations closed	*Date*
Reepham	1 November 1965
Langworth	1 November 1965
Snelland	1 November 1965
Wickenby	1 November 1965
Claxby & Usselby	7 March 1960
Holton-le-Moor	1 November 1965
Moortown	1 November 1965
Brocklesby	4 October 1993

Newark—Lincoln

Company   Midland Railway

Station closed	*Date*
Thorpe-on-the-Hill	7 February 1955